Elizabeth Hagen is professional, confidential, nonjudgmental, and extremely fun to work with! She has helped me take the chaos out of my life and replaced it with confidence, control, and peace of mind which are priceless!

–Senator Barbara Everist

It's Your Time!

This book is not just about organizing—it's about you. It's about developing confidence in yourself as you quickly become organized.

Just do a search on Google or Amazon or walk through your local book store and you will see lots of books about getting organized. There are also many books on self-esteem. Many of them are very good and provide a lot of information. But that's the catch—they may contain so much information that they just sit in your bookcase, unread. Someone who needs to get organized is already overwhelmed, and the last thing she needs is information overload.

That's where this book comes in. My goal is

to share strategies you can quickly learn and implement. Read the strategy, and within a few minutes you are actually organizing the area that has irritated you for so long!

You do for others all day long. Now it's time to take action and do something that will make every area of your life extraordinary. You've put this off long enough—it's your time! You are the CEO of your life!

About Elizabeth Hagen

"You *can* experience the joy of working in an environment that enables you to succeed and be *extraordinary!* "says Elizabeth Hagen, author, speaker, and professional organizer.

Elizabeth's humor, enthusiasm, honesty, and common sense have encouraged thousands of professionals to put her proven strategies and practical tips into action to help them not only *get* organized, but *stay* organized and feel fantastic!

Elizabeth's workshops, books, and tele-seminars help everyone from the "mildly messy" to the "desperately disorganized" save time, money, and frustration—and have fun while they do it.

Elizabeth has been married for over 27 years to her best friend, Dr. Bruce Jon Hagen, the best chiropractor in the nation. They have five fabulous children and live in peaceful South Dakota!

Elizabeth has spent the past 25 years developing systems and tools to make your life easier. She is a popular speaker at conferences, association meetings, conventions, and retreats.

Elizabeth's Life Verse:

But he's already made it plain how to live, what to do, what God is looking for in men and women.

It's quite simple: Do what is fair and just to your neighbor, be compassionate and loyal in your love, and don't take yourself too seriously—take God seriously.

−Micah 6:8 (*The Message*)

About Elizabeth Hagen

"You *can* experience the joy of working in an environment that enables you to succeed and be *extraordinary!*" says Elizabeth Hagen, author, speaker, and professional organizer.

Elizabeth's humor, enthusiasm, honesty, and common sense have encouraged thousands of professionals to put her proven strategies and practical tips into action to help them not only *get* organized, but *stay* organized and feel fantastic!

Elizabeth's workshops, books, and tele-seminars help everyone from the "mildly messy" to the "desperately disorganized" save time, money, and frustration—and have fun while they do it.

Elizabeth has been married for over 27 years to her best friend, Dr. Bruce Jon Hagen, the best chiropractor in the nation. They have five fabulous children and live in peaceful South Dakota!

Elizabeth has spent the past 25 years developing systems and tools to make your life easier. She is a popular speaker at conferences, association meetings, conventions, and retreats.

Elizabeth's Life Verse:

But he's already made it plain how to live, what to do, what God is looking for in men and women.

It's quite simple: Do what is fair and just to your neighbor, be compassionate and loyal in your love, and don't take yourself too seriously—take God seriously.

–Micah 6:8 (*The Message*)

Elizabeth Hagen

Organize
with
Confidence

Simplify Your Life and
Make Every Moment Count!

Foreword by
Glenna Salsbury, CSP, CPAE
Speaker Hall of Fame
2005 Cavett Award Winner

© 2006 Elizabeth Hagen

First edition
ISBN 1-881099-48-2

Cover photo: Suzie O'Meara Hernes
www.definedimpressions.com
Cover design: Jessica Mitchem
Editor: Sammy Smith
Production: SPS Publications, Eustis, Florida

For additional copies of this book, contact—

Elizabeth Hagen Books
4400 Northridge Circle
Sioux Falls, South Dakota 57105
www.ElizabethHagen.com
www.OrganizewithConfidence.com
Printed in the United States of America

For
Bruce, Chris, Emily, Abby, Sean, and Micah

Because of all of you I realized that
I had better learn about getting organized. Because of all of your support
I can now share confidently what I
know with the world!

I love each of you and
thank God for you every day.

Contents

Foreword

By Glenna Salsbury, CSP, CPAE

Speaker Hall of Fame
2005 Cavett Award Winner

Dear Friend,

You hold in your hand a kind of magic wand. Within these pages you will discover practical tools for bringing order into your daily existence. You will become better equipped to face your most paralyzing fears and gain an entirely new dimension of self-confidence.

Your everyday life may currently be overwhelming every day! Elizabeth Hagen delivers the wisdom that empowers you to bring order out of your chaos. She gives you easy-to-use systems for making your life make sense—personally and practically.

You will be encouraged as you discover Elizabeth's own journey to enjoyment in life. She speaks to you from her thirty years of learning the keys to confidence and creative living. You will find yourself eagerly peeking ahead to chapters yet unread. Her passion for your liberation is compelling.

Personal joy in living unfolds one day at a time. If you are on overwhelm your joy factor may be missing. Don't waste one more day. Give yourself the gift of dreaming new dreams. Take hold of the tools that will transform your surroundings. Your life will take on new meaning and fulfillment.

Elizabeth Hagen is a woman of character who has created a life that works, both balanced and purposeful. She has learned through personal experience the essential keys for overcoming her own fears and living with confidence. The results are visible in her love for her family, in her faith in God and in her fervor for the well-being of others.

I am blessed to know Elizabeth as both friend and colleague. You will be blessed to know her as well. Her life will transform yours as you turn these pages. Almost magically!

Warmly,
Glenna Salsbury
Author of *The Art of The Fresh Start*
February, 2006

Read This First!

I am so glad that you are holding this book. Congratulations! You are making a commitment to getting organized and to changing your life. And very soon, you will realize what a smart move you made!

This book is written for you. This is your guide to becoming a CEO—Confident – Efficient – Organized!

I am known for getting people to take action to have a better life, and that's exactly what I'm going to help you to do.

If you're feeling overwhelmed I understand. I know what it's like to feel overwhelmed by life, by all there is to do, and by all the people needing you. And I know what it's like to feel overwhelmed by circumstances absolutely out of our control and to feel like there is no hope.

I'd much rather be in charge of my life (at least as much as I can be) and take action to achieve my goals—wouldn't you? When I feel in control I feel better about myself. I'm more confident. I definitely treat others in my life much better *and* get much more accomplished.

Maybe some people are born confident but I definitely wasn't. Growing up, I was tall, skinny, shy, and to make matters worse, I stuttered. I didn't have low self esteem, I had NO self esteem. I've worked very hard at developing confidence and I discovered the following formula that changed my life:

Continue to Learn
Only You Can Change Anything
Notice Your Surroundings
Face the Fear and Do It Anyway
Imagine the Best
Dare to Have Big Goals
Establish Systems
Never Give Up
Compare Yourself Only to Yourself
Enjoy Life!

Perhaps you can relate to my story. But what about as adults? Life events happen that chip away at our self confidence, things people do to us damage our self confidence, and decisions that we've made that perhaps in hindsight were mistakes—whittle away at our confidence.

What are some things that have happened in your life that made you doubt your value?

_____

_____

_____

_____

Feeling out of control in our life can also tear down our confidence. Perhaps you feel totally out of control with the chaos in your home and office. Take heart! I'll teach you the tools to not only develop confidence but to gain control over your home, office, and your life.

You are a person of GREAT value, and I'm so glad that we can do this together!

Let's cut through all the "stuff" and get right

to the the tools you need to be Confident—Efficient—and Organized today!

If you're like me you jump around instead of reading a book from start to end. However, I strongly recommend that you read this little book from start to finish *first*. Then go back, and with the information that you received from Chapter 6 (Dare to Dream Big Goals), take action on your first goal.

Now, I know that you still may want to dig in right away. If so, here are some areas where you may want to take a quick peek:

You'll notice that I mention various forms throughout the book. In the *Organize with Confidence Manual* you will find all the forms along with a CD so you can download them to your computer.

At the end of each chapter is a Next Action section where I want you to write the action you are going to take as a result of reading that chapter. In your manual there is also an "Actions I Want to Take' form where you can record all the actions in one place.

I am so excited and honored that you have purchase my little book on being confident, efficient, and organized! It's small but it will definitely change your life. I'd love to hear from you!

– Elizabeth Hagen

Elizabeth@OrganizeWithConfidence.com
www.OrganizeWithConfidence.com
www.ElizabethHagen.com

People become really quite remarkable when they start thinking that they can do things. When they believe in themselves, they have the first secret of success.

— Norman Vincent Peale

Life is not easy for any of us. But what of that? We must have perseverance and above all confidence in ourselves. We must believe that we are gifted for something and that this thing must be attained.

— Marie Curie

Chapter One

Continue to Learn

Organizing is what you do before you do something,
so that when you do it, it is not all mixed up.

— A. A. Milne, Winnie-the-Pooh

I don't care if you have a high school education, college degree, or a P.h.D.—the end of formal education is the beginning of life-long learning. Never stop learning. Always be reading a book, taking a class or a teleclass, attending seminars.

List here any books, CDs, courses, etc. that you have been wanting to take, listen to, or do:

1.

2.

3.

4.

Since you have this book in your hands it shows me that you are a life-long learner. Congratulations! I want you to start learning right away so I'm going to teach you my START™ method of getting organized.

You may be a little wary since there's a good chance that you tried to get organized in the past and it didn't work. There are many reasons why this happened, but that's in the past. I am giving you systems that are proven. I'm also giving you decision-making processes so you won't ever just put something "here for now" anymore!

THE START™ METHOD

I was not always organized. Believe me, everything that I teach and help clients with I had to learn. I developed The START™ method after I had four children in five years. Suddenly life wasn't as simple as it once was! I knew I needed to gain control over my home and my life.

I found that when I was stressed I didn't treat people in my life the way I wanted to treat them nor as well as they deserved to be treated. I wanted to be the best mom and Family CEO™ that I could, but where could I get some guidance? There weren't many organization books out at that time and no such thing as a Google search, but somehow I found a few resources and started applying what I learned. Amazingly, as my environment started functioning better I felt more in control. I felt better about myself which made a huge difference in my life. This stuff really works!

The START™ method is a simple five-step organizing process that works in every area of your life. Pretty soon you'll be using it without even thinking about it!

START™ METHOD

S = Sort

T = Throw (or give, recycle, shred)

A = Appoint a home

R = Restrict to a container

T = Take back control

OK, let's do this. Go to your kitchen junk drawer or your desk drawer that holds all the pens, pencils, etc., and take everything out of the drawer—*everything*. If you don't take everything out, you are rearranging or cleaning, but you are not organizing. Put all the items on the desk or kitchen counter.

Now we'll begin the START™ method.

Sort/Toss

A high quality of life has a lot more to do with what you remove from your life than what you add to it.

—Cheryl Richardson

Start sorting through all the items. Ask yourself the following questions:

"Do I want to keep it?"
"Does it belong here?"
"Should I give it away?"
"Do I even know what it is?"

Do you see something that's broken or you don't need? Toss, recycle, or shred.

Do you see something that belongs somewhere else in the home or office? Do not leave! Draw an imaginary circle around your feet called the "Elizabeth Circle." You are not allowed to leave this circle until you are done organizing this drawer. When you find things that belong elsewhere put them in a box, and when you're finished with the drawer, put those items where they belong.

You are sorting and tossing at the same time. Get ruthless! Don't have any idea what this key is for?—toss. Have enough Post-it Notes? Give them to someone else in the office.

Appoint a Home

What's left after you've sorted and tossed is what actually belongs in that drawer. You have now "appointed a home" for these items. From now on, whenever you see that stapler out around the office you know it belongs in this drawer. It's amazing that when there are "homes" for items, you and others will put things away. How can you put anything away when you don't know where it goes?

Restrict to a Container

As much as possible put the items that belong in that drawer in containers. I like to purchase interlocking drawer bins that fit well in desk and kitchen drawers. Put all the pens together, paper clips together, etc.

Take Back Control

Look in this drawer. Wow! It's beautiful! Notice how you feel about yourself. You feel better because you've taken back control of an area in your life that's been bugging you.

Since you're not perfect this drawer will get messy again. It's OK. Take a breath and do the START™ method again. Every time you do this, it gets easier.

What I want you to take from this chapter...

Realize that the START™ method works everywhere: office, supply room, garage, closet. Anywhere you have areas that irritate you, take action and use the START™ method. Yes, it really is that easy!

I've used the START™ method with hundreds of clients. I love seeing the stress evaporate as I explain the system and we start working. As we're taking items out and making decisions, it's true that the area gets worse before it gets better. But as we continue working, clients become almost giddy as they see what they don't need leaving their life as they make room for what is important to them.

You will feel your confidence starting to rise when you start taking care of areas which have been irritating you for so long.

Next Action:

What area in your home or office do you want to begin the START™ method? You don't need to start organizing until you've read more of the book. I just want you to start thinking about where you'd like to start!

Chapter Two
Only You Can Change Anything

One can never change the past, only the hold it has on you, and while nothing in your life is reversible, you can reverse it nonetheless. –Merle Shain

I think one of the biggest epidemics in America (along with paper pile-up which we will take care of later!) is the "blame game." Nothing seems to be anybody's responsibility. Have you noticed this?

Do you have a tendency to blame things that are happening today on the past? It's time to stop blaming the past for the mistakes that you're making today. Living in the past keeps you stuck so you can't move forward.

Did you grow up in a home that was basically a disaster, so now you tell yourself you don't know how to be organized? Or were you raised in a home that was spotless, so now you are rebelling? How's that working for you? Chances are, it's not.

Start realizing that you are responsible for the life that you're living AND for the life that you want. This is extremely freeing! No more waiting for someone else to make you happy. It's up to you, and you can do it!

Focus

It's important to stay in the present and focus on what's happening now so you can make changes in your life.

Focus means doing something and thinking about it at the same time. Usually we are doing *this*—and thinking about *that*.

The Right Now Technique is a great technique to use to stay focused.

I first started using this technique back in 1988. I was running errands with our fourth child who was three, and about eight blocks from our house, the van died. Now this was before cell phones! I started to stress out about how I was going to get the van fixed, how was I going to take care of the rest of the errands that day, and pick up the other three children. I decided the best thing to do was to walk home with Sean and then call the car dealership. Still stressed, I started walking home. All of a sudden I looked around and realized it was a beautiful day, and I was holding the hand of the most adorable three-year-old in the entire world! I thought to myself, "Right now, I'm going to focus on this time with Sean and let the rest of the day work itself out." I did just that. Sean and I had a wonderful walk home as I listened to his chatter and thought to myself, "Life is good!"

That was a turning point for me. Now, whenever I start to feel stressed I stop and think, "Right now, what can I focus on and take care of?"

Right now, I hope you are focusing on what you are reading and thinking about how this simple mental technique can totally change your life. I mean totally!

Next time you feel stress, *focus*—it works!

Next Action:

Things I'm going to start taking responsibility for and make changes:

1.

2.

3.

4.

Chapter Three
Notice Your Surroundings

If I acquire as much as a stone, it owns me because I will have to dust it.

—Henry David Thoreau

We can get so used to our clutter that we think we don't notice it, but subconsciously it has a great impact. We don't think it's costing us or bothering us, but it is inside, emotionally. It's tearing down our self-confidence.

How do you feel when you look at your stacks of paper? How do you feel when you're afraid to open a closet door because you might get struck by an avalanche?

The first thing clutter costs is *time*. That's

obvious. If you're racing around trying to find things, your clutter is costing you time.

The second thing it costs is *energy*. Not only physical energy as you're racing around but more importantly, it's costing emotional energy.

Let's say you're on the phone with someone. They're asking for some information that it's your responsibility to have. You know you have it because you've *seen it somewhere*. You have no idea where, but you know that it's somewhere.

You have the phone crooked between your shoulder and your ear. With both hands, you're going though all the stacks of paper. You can't find it. You know you're not going to find it.

You get a sinking feeling in your stomach and sweat forms on your brow. At this point, are you calling yourself good names or pretty bad ones? Pretty bad ones, I'd guess. Your clutter is costing you emotional energy.

The third thing is *money*. Here's another scenario. You go to the grocery store without a list. You're in the mustard aisle. You think,

"Mustard? I think I have some. No, I don't. Yes, I do. Well, you just never know. I'll just buy some, and then I'll be safe."

You go home and for once, you really, really dig in your pantry. You find two bottles of mustard in the back. You haul them out and take off the lids. That black crust has formed at the top. They're old and beyond their expiration date, so you throw them out. Your clutter just cost you money.

The fourth thing it costs you *peace of mind*. If you shudder when someone rings your doorbell or comes to your office, then your clutter is costing you peace of mind. It's time to do something about it.

Look around you. What are your areas of irritation? Do you walk into your closet and get stressed? Are you tired of looking for things in stacks of paper? Really take the time to go through your home and office and notice which areas cause stress. Write them down here. We're going to organize these areas later.

1.

2.

3.

4.

5.

It's amazing how quickly your self-esteem grows when you take care of things in your life that have been bugging you for a long time.

I did a survey of all my newsletter subscribers to find out what stops them from getting organized. The overwhelming answer was that they didn't know where to start and they felt overwhelmed. That really hit me because I don't like feeling overwhelmed. I wanted to help others get rid of that feeling, too. I developed these simple steps to chunk down what may seem like an impossible situation.

Read through these steps first and then go back and do the steps in order. You are going to feel great!

7 Steps to Stop Feeling Overwhelmed

Step 1–Get Ready!

Get out your calendar or use the one provided in the *Organize with Confidence* manual and pick the date when you'll go through your entire house or office. Depending on the size of your house/office/apartment, this will take about 30 minutes to 2 hours. (You'll just be planning what needs to be organized—you won't necessarily start organizing on that day.)

Make extra copies of the Room Forms from the manual as needed. Be sure to copy enough for your home or office.

When the day arrives for you to go through your home or office, put on your favorite music and get ready to have some fun!

Have your forms on a clipboard with you with pen in hand.

Step 2—Identify the Areas to Organize!

Begin at your front door/office door with your pen and Room Forms (found in the manual).

Imagine a big clock imposed on the floor. Choose where you want 12 o'clock. You can also think of it as North, South, East and West.

Start at 12 o'clock and begin circling clockwise. As soon as you see an area that you're tolerating or that bothers you, write it down on the Room Form.

Keep circling the room until you're back at 12 o'clock, writing every area down that needs attention.

Before you leave the room, look at your list

and put a star by the area you want to work on first. (Don't put more than 1—2 stars per room.)

Great! You're done with this room! Now go on to the next room.

Step 3–Prioritize

Sit down at your desk or kitchen table with the Priority and Assign Form found in the manual.

Go through each Room Form you filled out and transfer the areas you put a star by onto the Priority Form. (Just list them all for now—you don't have to put them in order of most important yet.)

Once you've listed all the areas from all the rooms, you can prioritize them by what you want to get done first, second, third, etc.

Step 4–Choose a Date

On the same Priority and Assign Form, write the name of the person responsible for the task.

Next, set a date you'll work on that area and put it in your calendar.

Step 5—Get Ready to Take Action

Take your number one priority off your Priority Form and write it onto your Take Action Form.

Determine what supplies you'll need. (See Suggested Tools Sheet found in the Appendix.)

Write the date down that you've decided to work on that area.

If you like, you can break down the area into smaller tasks. For example:

"Purchase hanging file folders."

"Get garbage bags out."

"Make sure kids are with the sitter."

"Take day off from work."

"Gather cleaning supplies."

"Make space on floor to empty things."

Then write the reward you'll give yourself when you're done!

Step 6—Do it!

Post the START™ sign near where you're working.

Optional: You can also post the Guideline for Quality Living and Clutter definition sheets from the manual for additional support.

Get out your Working Signs from the manual:

"Take to other area"
"Keep"
"Give"
"Garage Sale"
"Throw"
"Fix/Alterations"

Put the Working Signs by appropriate bags and/or boxes.

Take everything out of the area you're going to organize and begin using the START™ method (explained in Chapter One).

Step 7—Reward, Relax and Repeat

Well done! Acknowledge yourself and enjoy what you've just accomplished.

Be sure and give yourself your reward!

Cross this task off your Priority Form!

If you choose, you can keep going and go to the next priority, fill out a Take Action Form for that area, and do it!

What I want you to take from this chapter...

Have you picked an area to start, but you feel totally overwhelmed and want to run? That's perfectly normal. Read through the 7 Steps again and believe in the process. This works—just START!

When someone hears that I'm a Professional Organizer and that along with my speaking, I work one-on-one with professionals in their home or offices, one of the most frequent comment I hear is, "I need you to come to my office but I'm too embarrassed to have you see my mess!"

My reply is, "I see solutions, not the problem!"

That's what I'm giving you in this book. I'm giving you solutions—the tools to solve your organizing issues. Follow the 7 Steps, use the START™ method and trust the process. It works!

Next Action:

Decide the date you are going to start the 7 Steps in your home or office:

Date: _____

Chapter Four

Face Your Fear and Do It Anyway

You gain strength, courage, and confidence by every experience in which you really stop to look fear in the face. You must do the thing, which you think you cannot do.

—Eleanor Roosevelt

Anytime we do something out of our comfort zone, it's normal to feel fear and perhaps even panic. When this happens, think about it. Really think about it. Is it a valid fear? Are you in danger? Or is it a fear that it totally in your mind? If you can overcome it, can you achieve your goal? Go forward if it's in your head. Usually FEAR stands for: Fantasized Evidence Appearing Real.

When I first started my business I knew I needed to get my name out but didn't have a budget for advertising. My thought was to contact the local TV stations and be a guest on early morning shows and give organizing hints. I thought about it for over a year! My fear of—what if I say something dumb?, what if they say no?, and what if I look foolish? kept me from calling the station. I finally decided that my fear was not real. I called them and the TV station was glad to have me as a guest. Now I love being on TV, and I am so glad that I faced my fear and did it anyway!

Your fear may be that you've tried to get organized before and it didn't work. In my opinion that fear is totally in your head and not valid. You will now have the tools. That fear is in the past—let's move forward.

Two traps that fear uses to keep us stuck are procrastination and perfectionism.

Procrastination
A task left undone remains left undone in two places—at the actual location of the task, and inside

your head. Incomplete tasks in your head consume the energy of your attention as they gnaw at your conscience. They siphon off a little more of your personal power every time you delay. No need to be a perfectionist, that's dehabilitating in an imperfect world, but it's good to be a 'completionist'. If you start it, finish it—or forget it. –Brahma Kumaris

When you procrastinate, you are living life by constantly stepping on your brakes. Common reasons heard from procrastinators are: This will take too long, I don't know how to do this, I'm overwhelmed and don't know where to start.

Procrastination Solutions

1. Visualize how you will feel when you accomplish this task that you are putting off.
2. Break the task down into steps.
3. Make an appointment with yourself to do this task and KEEP the appointment.
4. Take action.
5. Give yourself a great reward.

Use the Procrastination worksheet in the

manual to write down what you are procras-
tinating on and what action you will now
take.

Perfectionism

*I'm careful not to confuse excellence with perfec-
tion. Excellence I can achieve, perfection is God's
business.* –Michael J. Fox

Perfectionism is another very common
trap. We never feel satisfied with how we are
doing on a project. We feel, "If I keep working at this, I'll come up with a better idea or
a different way." This keeps us from getting
anything done. Give up perfectionism and
focus on mastery instead!

Perfectionism Solution:

1. Put the task in perspective. How many
   do-overs will really make a difference? Tell
   yourself that you will work on this two
   more times and then it's going to be good
   enough.
2. Give yourself a clear deadline to get it

done.

3. Reward yourself for the effort, not the result.

What I want you to take from this chapter...

Really think next time you feel fear. Is it valid? Is there real reason for concern? Or is it just your perfectionism or procrastination taking over?

Next Action:

Name a big fear in your life and write it here:

_____

_____

Is it valid?

Yes _____ No _____

Chapter Five

Imagine the Best

For as he thinks in his heart, so is he...
—Proverbs 23:7a

Charles Swindoll wrote: "The longer I live, the more I realize the impact of attitude on life. Attitude to me is more important than facts. It is more important than the past, than education, than money, than circumstances, than failures, than success, than what other people think or say or do. It is more important than appearance, gift, or skill. It will make or break a company...a church...a home. The remarkable thing is we have a choice every day regarding the attitude we will embrace for that day. We cannot change our past...we cannot change the fact that people will act in a certain way. We cannot change the inevitable. The only thing we can do is play on the string we have, and that is our attitude. I am convinced that life is 10 percent what happens to me and 90 percent how I react to it. And so it is with you... we are in charge of our attitudes."

This is so true! But how can we use this fact to make a difference? Begin to learn the art of positive thinking. When you start thinking positively, positive things happen. It's truly amazing!

If you look at your clutter and think, "I'm such a failure. Why can't I get organized? How did my life get to be such a mess?"—believe me, nothing is going to happen.

Think instead, "This clutter is limiting my life. I know that I can take care of this." You will start to see the area to start and begin taking steps to gain control back. You must visualize success before it happens.

When you do the "7 Steps to Stop Feeling Overwhelmed" method from Chapter Three, it's very important to write down how you visualize the room will look after it's organized. (Write this on the bottom of the Room Form.) This is a great example of "Imagining the Best!"

I tend to be a naturally negative thinker. I really have to work at thinking positively. What has helped me is that I have worked very hard at getting negative, draining people out of my life.

I was visiting with a major client the other day and commented that everyone in his company was so nice. He replied, "I only hire nice people."

I asked him, "But what if someone is mean?"

He replied with an absolutely straight face, "I fire them!"

What a concept! Who do you need to fire from your life? I've fired banks, retail stores, and friends, just to name a few.

Next Action:

Start listening to what you say to yourself. What do you beat yourself up about? My

husband calls it, "Stinking Thinking!" Reframe
your "stinking thinking" thought and write it
here as a positive statement:

Chapter Six

Dare to Have Big Goals

How different our lives are when we really know what is deeply important to us, and keeping that picture in mind, we manage ourselves each day to be and to do what really matters most.

—Stephen Covey

You can dream as big as you want to—what's to stop you? The only thing that might stop you is yourself. You may not think that you deserve your dreams or that you have the ability to achieve them. But you do! I'm living proof that goals work, and I know they will work for you.

Would you dream of driving across the

country without a map or a GPS system? I hope not! It's the same with our life. How can we know where we want to end up if we don't have a plan or what I call a GPS—Goal Planning System?

Goals are dreams written down. They start becoming real when you put them on paper. I started my business because of a dream I had years ago which I wrote down and looked at every day until it became a reality.

If you're not sure of even where to begin to set goals the Life Balance Wheel may help. Use the Life Balance Wheel template in the manual or draw a large circle on a piece of paper with seven wedges. Label them Business/Career, Contribution, Financial, Fun, Health/Spiritual, Personal, and Relationship.

Business/Career

Are you happy with your career? What do you really want to be doing every day career wise?

Contribution

Are you involved as much as you'd like to be with the community and charity projects?

Financial

How content are you with your financial status? This is nothing to do with how much money you have, but your contentment with your finances.

Fun

Yes, fun! What activities would you like to try?

Health/Spiritual

Are you happy with your spiritual life? What mental and physical habits do you need to work on?

Personal

Are there skills you'd like to master and items you'd like to own? What vacations would you like to take?

Relationship

Are you spending enough time with family and friends?

Now you are going to rate your level of contentment in each area of your life. If you are extremely content in that area put a dot on that line near the outside of the circle, if you are not content put the dot near the center of the circle. When you've rated each area of your life connect the dots with a line.

You will now see your current life balance. Are you surprised? You can see at a glance which areas need extra effort and you may want to set goals in those areas first.

It's a good idea to do the Life Balance Wheel every three months and see where you've made progress and where you may need to make some adjustments.

Getting Started

Now let's set some goals and start making your dreams come true! How? Just START!

Specific

This is not the time be vague—be specific.

Timely

Set a start date and completion date for your goal.

Action steps

Break the goal down into actions steps so it won't seem so hard to achieve.

Realistic

Goal needs to be realistic—challenging, but realistic.

True for you

Your goals need to be what you want to accomplish—not what someone else says you should do.

It's imperative that you write down your goals as positive statements, as if it has already happened. Change the statement, "I'd like to make more money" to "I am making $120,000 this year."

I highly recommend taking the time later to set goals for each of the life areas but for the purposes of this book take out the Personal and Business/Career Goal Worksheets in the manual. Look back under letter N—Notice Your Surroundings. Do you have areas of irritation at home, office, or both? Write those areas down as a goal on the appropriate worksheet. If it's your office your goal might be, "I work in an organized and efficient environment," and you would write that on your Business/Career Goal Worksheet.

If your goal is to have a closet where only clothes you love live you would write, "I walk into my closet each morning and can pick from clothes that I love." You would write that on your Personal Goal Worksheet. Later in the book you'll find out EXACTLY how to achieve those goals.

Notice that these goals are stated in the positive as if they have already happened. This is very important!

What I want you to take from this chapter...

Stop confusing goals with New Year's resolutions. They are not the same thing. Often, New Year's resolutions are made because someone else thought you should change something in your life.

I like what Mark Victor Hansen calls goals—"To Do Lists with Deadlines!"

Your goals are just for you. Don't skip taking action on this chapter! Your goals will change your life.

Next Action:

Take the time now to write out your goals on the goal sheets in the manual. What is the first goal you are going to start working on?

_____

_____

Chapter Seven

Establish Systems

What the world really needs is more love and less paper work. –Pearl Bailey

If you walk into your office and feel a sense of desperation, this chapter is for you. It's time to set up systems that work for you.

Systems are very important in life. Think of the stoplight system. What a mess we'd have if we didn't have structure at an intersection.

When you have systems you will:
Save
Yourself
Stress
Time
Energy and
Money

What's important with organizing systems is that any system you use has to be easier than what you already have. If not, you won't do it. You also need to understand that any system does require some work on your part. There is no system that will function by itself and keep you organized! Sad but true!

I feel that paper pile-up is the latest national epidemic, so I'm going to devote this chapter to teaching you systems to handle all the paper—whether at home or in the office.

The Wall Street Journal reported: "The average U.S. executive wastes 6 weeks annually searching for misplaced information from messy desks and files. (That translates to five hours per week, or one hour per day. At $65,000 per year in salaries, that's nearly $8,125,000 per year wasted time on the job.)"

Would you like to calculate the bottom-line impact of disorganization for your company? Use the calculator at my website by visiting www.ElizabethHagen.com/calculator.html.

When you walk into the office and look at all those stacks of paper do you feel hopeless?

Chances are, instead of getting to work you check your e-mail or get a cup of coffee—anything but face the nightmare on your desk.

What if you could walk into your office and feel good, because on your desk is the most important thing to do that morning, and you know where the important papers are to work on? Think of how good you'd feel about yourself and the time you'll save. Think about how much more productive you would be which means—you are going to make more money!

What if someone called you and asked for some information—and you knew exactly where to go and get it because it's at your fingertips? Wouldn't that be a fantastic feeling? Of course, and it would raise your self-confidence, too. It would make you a better boss, employee or business owner, and person.

The Three Decisions

There are only three decisions to make with a peice of paper. You can either Toss the paper, Act on it, or put it in a Reference File. There is *no* stuffing, stacking, or spreading! Look at your desk. Your stuffing, stacking, and spreading got you into this mess in the first place. You had no choice. Without a decision-making process the natural tendency is to stuff, stack, or spread.

Have you heard the saying, "Touch a piece of paper only once?" It's a myth. That is only true with Charmin or Kleenex!

It's okay to touch it more than once, but you need to make one of the three decisions. It's amazing how the decisions will organize your office and keep you on top of all your paperwork.

We are going to focus on paper in this chapter, but the same decisions are true for voicemail, e-mail, verbal requests, and the things you think about.

Toss

The first step is toss—and I also mean shred or recycle. We keep more paper than necessary, so get rid of what you don't need. Ask yourself some basic questions:

- Can I get this paper easily somewhere else? If yes, get rid of it

- Does this paper require any action? If it does, set it aside. I'll address the action papers later in this chapter.

- Is there a specific use for this piece of paper? If not, throw it.

- Is this the most recent copy? If yes, then keep it.

- Are there tax or legal considerations? Here's where someday/maybe works. If you're not sure, keep the paper.

- If I discard this paper and need it again someday, what's the worst thing that would happen to me? If you can live with the answer get rid of the paper.

Act Now

If you can't toss it, you may need to act on it. My guideline is if it takes two minutes or less, just do it, get it done. Hopefully you can toss it after you've completed the action.

Act —Delegate

Perhaps it needs action but someone else could do it. Ask yourself, "Is it something that has to be done by me?" We need to start putting more value on our time. If, for example, you're worth $100 an hour, and this paper needs to be filed, give it to your $10 an hour assistant to file it for you.

Here are the steps to delegate so the job will get done:
1. Pick the right person for the job.
2. Be very clear about what you want done.
3. Verify that they understand.
4. Set a deadline.
5. Get their agreement.

Use the Delegation Log in the manual to stay on top of the tasks that you've given to someone else.

Act Later

If it's an action that has to be done by you

but will take some time, it is an Act Later decision. This is very important to understand. Most of the papers on your desk and on your floor fall into the Act Later category. The papers are there because you knew you needed to take some action, but you didn't put them away. Why? Because you were afraid you'd forget to do it and not be able to find it again. Meanwhile, the papers get lost anyway because you stack more things on top.

For some of the actions you could just make a notation in your calendar system and then toss the paper. But for those papers you want to keep as reminders, I have a great system for you. It's called, the Vital Files System, so you will have a "home" for these papers until you have time to do the action.

Vital Files System

- Folders 1 – 31
- Folders January – December

Permanent Action Folders:
- Awaiting Reply

- Casual Reading
- Coupons/Gift Certificates
- Data Entry
- Reminder Forms
- Goals
- Meetings
- People
- Purchases/Errands
- Take Home
- To File

Vital Files

I call this system the Vital Files System because they are essential to every office.

You're going to get 31 hanging file folders labeled 1 through 31 and 12 more labeled January through December. You will find the label template in the manual.

Vital Files Drawer

The Vital Files go in the file drawer closest to where you sit. In most cases if you're right-handed that is the lower right hand drawer.

This drawer needs to be a swivel away from your chair—not a swivel and a push. You're going to be in and out of these folders all day long.

How to Use the Files

Always ask yourself, "When do I need to see this piece of paper again in order to get it done when it's due?"

If you get a piece of paper that reminds you to call Mary by the twelfth, put that piece of paper in the 12th folder and forget about it.

When the twelfth day of the month comes, take all the papers out of that folder and you'll have everything that you need to do that day.

If something comes up that you don't have to take care of until December, you're going to put it in the December folder.

The key to this system is to check it every day. I like to plan for the day the night before. Every night I pull out the files for the next day and put them on my desk because I know those are things I need to do.

Examples

Let's say you're going to go to a concert in two weeks. Where do you put the tickets? Put them in the date of the concert.

Do you have a birthday coming up? If you've bought the card already, put it in the dated folder for the day you want to mail it. It's ready to go.

This system is great for bills, too. Just know that if you mail a bill it takes five days to get to the receiver so if the bill is due the 20th put it in the 15th folder.

It's great for contact follow-up for clients. If you want to visit or call them next week, make a note and drop it in next week's folder.

If you're going to go on a trip and you've printed out a map with MapQuest, put the directions in the date you're going to travel. When I fly by air I always have my itinerary and my confirmation number all in the dated folder on the day I will travel. The morning I travel I just take the information out of that folder, and I'm ready to go.

That's the beauty of the system. It's ready to go and you won't forget. The other beauty is it'll never run out of batteries or crash.

Prioritize

When you use the Vital Files System you can very easily prioritize your day because everything you need to do that day is in one spot. Take everything out of today's folder and spread it out on your desk. Look at all the tasks and ask yourself, "What is the most important use of my time right now?" Take that piece of paper and turn it over.

Next ask yourself, "What's the second most important use of my time?" Take that paper and turn it over. Keep going until all the papers are all turned upside down.

Then turn the pile over and your day is prioritized—and it probably only took you less than a minute. You will now work on that first item until it is completed. Do not check your e-mail or get a cup coffee. Focus on that first action, then reward yourself when it's accomplished.

Permanent Action Folders

Along with the 1-31 and Monthly folders you will have permanent action folders as part of the Vital Files System.

Awaiting Reply— when you've called someone and left a message, fill out a Reminder Form and drop it in here. Check this file three to four times a day.

Casual Reading—put only casual reading here and take this folder when you go on a trip or to the doctor's office. For any business reading, you should pick a day and drop it in the Vital Files System.

Coupons/GC—put coupons, carry-out menus, gift certificates, etc. here.

Data Entry—When you come back to the office with some business cards or contact information, put it in this folder until you have time to enter them into your Contact System.

Reminder Forms—place blank Reminder Forms here (form found in the manual). Use this form whenever you have an idea you want to do, to record a message you've received or to remind you that you left a phone message with someone. Also use it for follow-up with someone to whom you've delegated a task. Have plenty of copies in the Reminder Forms folder.

Goals—for ideas of things you want to do someday. Check this one monthly.

Meetings—make a labeled folder for any regular meetings—weekly, monthly, etc. and put any papers here that you want to discuss at the meeting.

People—make a label for your boss, spouse and anyone else you deal with on a daily basis. When they call or stop by your office you will have what you need to talk to them about in one place. For people you deal with occasionally just drop any paper that you need to talk to them about in a certain day in the Vital Files System.

Purchases/Errands—put a small spiral notebook in here and keep track of what you need to purchase when you're out.

Take Home—put papers here that you want to take home.

To File—keep papers here to put in a reference file and empty it weekly.

Make Checking the Vital Files a New Habit

"Motivation is what gets you started. Habit is what keeps you going." –Jim Rohn

For this system to work you need to make it a habit to check it the same time each day. A great way to get used to doing this is to exchange an old habit for a new one. If it's your habit now to check your e-mail first thing, check the Vital Files instead. If it's your habit to get a cup of coffee first thing, check the Vital Files instead.

Reference File

We've now taken care of the Toss and Act part of the decision-making process. Any papers left are for your reference file. These are papers for which the action is complete, but you may need to reference them at some point in the future.

Examples of those particular files are your tax returns, insurance papers, titles and passports. Some of these things should go in a safe deposit box. Again, there's no further action needed, but you may need to refer to them later. This can be a real problem if you don't have a good filing system—and most people don't!

I have some options for you. If you want to set up the file system yourself be sure to use broad categories. If you get too specific, you are left with too many choices and you won't know where to file.

The other option is to use the brainchild of other people who have come up with some great systems.

Kiplinger's Taming the Paper Tiger™ Software System

If you like using the computer and are running a business, then the Paper Tiger Software System (www.SaveAnHouraDay.com) is for you. This is my choice, and I guarantee that if you use this system you can find anything you file or store in five seconds or less! Just imagine!

With this system you still file papers in file folders in a file cabinet but you catalog each folder in the easy-to-use database in the software system. When you want to find something, you just type in any keyword in the Google-like find feature and immediately you are told exactly where the paper is!

The Paper Tiger is a complete office organization kit including the filing system software, multimedia tutorial, time saving pre-printed file folder labels and online User's Guide. This includes organizing tips from professional organizers—everything you need to solve your paper filing problems once and for all!

The Paper Tiger System definitely benefited my client, Sarah. She had written over $1,000 in checks on four different accounts and put them in the mail box. Sometime during the night the entire mailbox was stolen. She had all the receipts carefully filed in her software system so it only took her 30 minutes to call everyone to tell them what had happened and to rewrite the necessary checks.

She had phone numbers and account information right where she needed it, instantly accessible. She told me before using this system she would spend at least that much time scrounging around her office just wondering what to do first.

Home Paper

Have you forgotten the color of your kitchen counter under where all the mail seems to end up? Have you stopped eating on the kitchen table because of the stacks of paper? Today is the day to set up your own Household Command Center so you can stop the piles of paper before they start. Many of the same principles you learned in the Office Paper section will apply here, but since there usually isn't a file drawer in the kitchen I will teach you how to set up a Household Command Center.

Household Command Center

Collect all the paper from the table and counter and let's get going!

Your Household Command Center is where you will keep all the paper that requires some action. Bills, soccer schedule, birthday cards to send out, etc. You're going to wonder how you lived without it!

Just like in the office, there are three decisions to make when you pick up a piece of paper: Can you toss it? Should you act on it? Or is the action completed and you want to file it away in case you'd need it later? I explained these decisions in detail earlier, but for now we're just going to deal with the papers you need to act on in the future. Their new home is the Household Command Center (picture in the manual).

Tools for the Household Command Center

- Desktop File Box
- Tickler File (www.TheTIcklerFile.com)
- Labeled colored hanging file folders (labels in manual)

Inside the front of the Desktop File Box put the Tickler File. This system has files labeled 1-31 and January through December. It's called a tickler file because it tickles your memory and reminds you to do things later.

You bring the mail in and there's a bill that's due on the 15th. You know that it takes five days to reach the recipient once you drop it in the mail. You go to the number 10 tab, put it behind there, and forget about it. You need to call Mary about something and you know she's back from vacation on the 20th—put the reminder behind the 20th tab and forget about it.

Information may arrive about camp for your kids this summer. You don't need to register until May, so put it behind the May tab. When May comes, pull everything out of May and put it under the correct date in May. If today is March 8, the 8th—31st tabs are March and tabs one through seven becomes April.

The second part of the Command Center is for things that don't need to be done on any certain date. Purchase yellow 1/5 cut hanging file folders and label them with labels for each family member along with Coupons, Errands, Order, Read, Receipts, School, Take to Office, To Do Now, and To File. You may have others depending on what's going on in your life right now. If you're the PTA president, be sure you have a PTA folder for all action papers you need to do with the PTA.

Teach your family members to check their folders daily. This will stop you from having to remember all of their stuff. Anything you need to discuss with them—put it in their folder, and they can look it over and get back to you.

This Command Center will miraculously take every piece of paper that is an action item off your kitchen counter. You will never forget anything again as long as you check the Command Center every day. Get yourself in the habit, every morning or night, of checking the folder for that day or the next day.

Family Notebook

The Family Notebook is a great tool for reference papers that you want to keep close by. You want to keep the school lunch schedule within reach, you'd like to see the Pilates schedule from the wellness center every few days, etc. The answer is the Family Notebook. In a three-ring binder have the following tabs: Phone, Home, Chores, School, Church, Finances, Computer, Travel, Goals, and a tab for each family member. All the forms for the notebook are in the manual.

Reference File

If you are going to file manually, just like in the office, use broad categories. In the manual I give you a list of common home reference filing categories.

HomeFile Financial Planning Kit

Since my mission is to make your life easier, I'm always on the lookout for great products that do just that. The HomeFile Financial Planning Kit (Appendix) is one of these products.

This kit is perfect if you do not have a home business and you are just filing for home use.

It comes with 23 tabbed laminated divider cards detailing exactly what to file behind this tab, what not to file behind the tab, and how long to keep it. Absolutely amazing and so easy to set up.

It goes even further. It comes with a handbook with easy instructions and forms that you and your spouse should fill out so that if anything ever happens to one of you—the other will know where the will is, who the attorney is, and where the life insurance policies are located.

Make an Appointment

Make an appointment in your calendar to organize your office—and KEEP the appointment!

I suggest that you start on top of your desk or kitchen counter first. That's where your most current items are. Then go to your floor, and lastly into your desk. Use the Vital File System or Household Command Center, the three decision process, and just go for it! Warning: working with paper is tedious and people get bored very fast. You might want to have an accountability partner or set your timer for an hour a day to work on this.

What I want you to take from this chapter...

There is hope for all the paper in your life,

but you just need to take time to set up the correct system. Utilize the three-decision process, the Vital Files System, and a good reference file system to make your life a LOT easier and get more done in less time.

Next Action:

Do you want to start with your home paper or office paper?

Home _____ Office _____

Purchase the supplies listed in the Appendix for either the Vital Files or the Household Command Center and make an appointment to get started.

Date to start: _____

On calendar? _____

Your whole life becomes more meaningful when you are organized because you are free to focus on others. **–Glenna Salsbury**

Chapter Eight
Never Give Up

Learn from the mistakes of others. You can't live long enough to make them all yourself. –Eleanor Roosevelt

Failure is as much a part of life as success. How else can we learn unless we make mistakes? I figure with five children I've made at least 5,000,000 mistakes, but I'm still a mom. So much of success is simply not giving up.

Winston Churchill once gave a commencement address for Oxford University. He got up to the lectern and said, "Never, never, never give up!" and then sat down. It was probably the shortest speech on record and the most profound advice these young people ever received.

It's also important not to give up just because you can't do it perfectly. I am a recovering perfectionist! I finally realized that there is no perfection this side of heaven and I started having my goal to be one of excellence instead of perfection. Let go of perfection and strive for excellence.

Mind Mapping

Perhaps you've tried getting organized before and it didn't work. So now you get down on yourself every time you look around and think, "I really need to get organized." Never give up!

Mind mapping is a wonderful tool to use to break large tasks down into chunks and see the light at the end of the tunnel. It's great to use if you tried to accomplish a task before and it didn't go well, and now you need a new way to look at it.

Mind mapping allows you to play with ideas creatively instead of getting stuck trying to logically record your ideas too soon in the idea-generating process.

When I help clients organize their office, we begin by mind mapping the entire room. When we get all the areas down on paper in the mind-mapping format, it is usually easy to tell which area we should start on and which areas are not significant problems.

Sometimes I have all kinds of thoughts racing around in my head about how to approach a particular project. Before I start, I simply sit down with my mind-mapping tools and take a deep breath. I use mind mapping to plot out the project step-by-step. Within minutes, I have a plan—and my confusion is gone.

How to Do a Mind Map
Step 1

Take a large, unlined piece of paper and draw a three-inch circle in the middle. Why the middle? It's much easier to allow yourself room to grow and work outward rather than inward.

Step 2

Inside the circle put your topic of the mind map. For example, if you are mind mapping to get your office organized you would put the word "office" in the circle. If you are mind mapping putting together a presentation, you would put the draft title of the presentation in the circle.

Step 3

Draw branches extending out from the circle. These will resemble roots of a tree as they expand at the base and narrow near the ends. Again, using the example of organizing an office, have a branch for each main area that you want to organize (i.e., desk, computer, floor, bookcase, file cabinet, etc.). Then create sub-branches off of each main branch. For example, the main branch heading of "desk" may include sub-branches such as top of desk, middle desk drawer, file drawer, etc.

Try to use the one-word-per-line rule for each branch. This may seem difficult at first, but is essential to learn because it helps us to refine the information before writing it down.

See the example at—
www.ElizabethHagen.com/officemindmap.

Step 4

Be creative and have fun! Use colored pencils and makers, draw pictures, and use stickers! Giving your mind map a bit of your personality will help make it uniquely yours.

Would you like a template to start your first mind map?

Go to—
www.ElizabethHagen.com/mindmaptemplate

You can be successful with mind mapping but you have to give it a try. Mind mapping is a great tool to help you become more focused, organized, and productive. Practice mind mapping by using it to plan the following types of projects:

• Planning your day

- Planning your week
- Goal setting
- Putting together a presentation
- Taking notes during a speech
- Recording highlights of a book
- Improve activities important to your success

Here's all you will need to get started:

- Unlined paper—preferably 11 x 17
- Felt-tip pens, markers, colors, stickers, colored pencils
- Highlighters
- Your brain
- Whatever else you need to personalize YOUR mind map!

The secret of getting ahead is getting started. The secret of getting started is breaking your complex overwhelming tasks in to small manageable tasks, and then starting on the first one. –Mark Twain

Chapter Nine
Compare Yourself Only to Yourself

No one can make you feel inferior without your consent.
–Eleanor Roosevelt

Women, in particular, are notorious for comparing themselves to others and then usually feeling bad about themselves. Someone is always going to have nicer clothes, a bigger home, and a better job. But this kind of thinking gets us nowhere—fast.

The first step is to come to an acceptance of how you were made. Short, wide, tall, broad shoulders—that's just the way it is. Aren't sure what styles are best for you? Image consultants are experts in knowing how to dress your body.

Invest with one and know that you can look the best just the way you are.

Be realistic. Is there something you don't like about yourself that you can change? Do it! Stop talking about it and take the steps.

Stop comparing. And, if you insist on comparing then compare yourself with yourself. Where were you at last year in your career? Where are you now? How were your relationships last year? How are they now? Need to make some changes? Go for it!

Start making these changes by getting clothes out of your life that make you feel bad. Yes, the clothes that don't fit and you know don't look good on you!

Organizing Your Closet

The average person wears 20% of the clothes in her closet. That means that 80% is just sitting there. When I ask my audiences why they don't wear 80% of their clothes they all say, "Because they don't fit!"

I then ask, "If they don't fit why are they in

your closet?"

"They might fit someday!" is the answer.

Think about that—it doesn't make any sense. If you really think you will be able to wear them again someday, take those clothes that don't fit and store them. There's absolutely no reason they have to take up room in your closet and cause you huge emotional distress, as well. Every time you bypass the jeans that are too small you're telling yourself that you don't like the way you are right now. That is wasted emotional energy.

Tools:
- Box for alterations
- Box for things that belong elsewhere in the home
- Garbage bag for toss items
- Garbage bag or box for give or garage sale items
- Good hangers
- 2-pocket folder with Shopping List from manual

6 Steps to an Organized Closet

Step 1: Clear off the floor and bed
Step 2: Take everything out of the closet
Step 3: Use the START™ method
Step 4: Put the clothing back
Step 5: Go shopping
Step 6: You did it!

Step 1: Clear off the floor and bed

You're going to need some room to work, so clear out what's on the floor and make your bed so you can lay clothes on the bed.

Step 2: Take everything out of the closet

Yes, everything! You will understand now when I say that things will look worse before they look better. As you're taking things out and you find items that belong elsewhere in the home do not leave! Remember the "Elizabeth Circle" from Chapter One! Just place these items in a box and take them away when you are done.

Step 3: Use the START™ method

Start going through the clothing and Sort and Toss/Give at the same time. Don't like it? Give or toss. Doesn't fit but you like it? Put in a storage bin to keep until that day arrives. Like it but it needs to be hemmed? Put in the alteration box.

My guideline is, "How do you feel when you put it on?"—not, "If you haven't worn it in a year then get rid of it." Does it make you feel pretty/handsome? Keep it even though you may not have worn it in 3 years. Do you feel tired and drained wearing it? Give it away even if it's only a month old.

Go through each piece of clothing and be absolutely ruthless. Try on whatever you're not sure of. You will be exhausted but the final outcome will be worth it!

As you're deciding if you want to keep an item or give it away, don't forget that there are so many people who could wear those clothes right now that you're keeping for whatever reason. Perhaps you don't even know why you're keeping them! It feels great to give to others.

One client had a wonderful way to help her give more clothes away. She made up an imaginary person named Aunt Matilda, and whenever we worked together she would say, "I think Aunt Matilda could use this." I'd smile and drop it in the give away bag. She would then take the bags to charity. She felt good about it because they were going to her imaginary Aunt Matilda!

You may want to keep a basket or bin in your closet for donated items for the future. It's easier to make the decision to give when the container is right in your closet.

Step 4: Put the clothes back

What is left now belongs in your closet. Start hanging the clothes back in categories. All blouses together, all pants together, etc. Inside each category, hang back by color. All whites, then pinks, blues, etc.

As you're hanging clothes back you are

doing the R—Restrict to a Container since the hanger is a container. You may also want to use baskets/bins for purses, hose, and accessories.

Keep a shopping list (from the manual) handy so you can keep notes of what you need. Yes, you get to go shopping when you're done if you've really been ruthless!

Step 5: Go Shopping!

Keep a two-pocket folder with the shopping list in it in your closet or dresser drawer. You could also use it for receipts of clothing that you've bought recently, coupons, or pictures of items that you like. When you're ready to go shopping you can take the folder with you.

Step 6: You Did It!

Now, look in your closet. It is a thing of beauty! Doesn't it feel great to finally clear out what you know you haven't wanted to keep in years? You have now just completed the T—Take Back Control.

I suggest going through your closet each spring to get ready for summer and each fall to get ready for winter.

What I want you to take from this chapter...

Gaining control of your home boils down to taking action steps. Decide which area you want to organize, set an appointment to organize this area, and do it! It's all about taking action. You've told yourself long enough that you need to do this—START today!

Next Action:

Pick a date and make an appointment with yourself to ruthlessly go through your closet.

Date: _____

Date Completed: _____

Donations Made: _____

_____

_____

Chapter Ten

Enjoy Life!

Smile and the world smiles with you.
—Ella Wheeler Wilcox

Smile! Be enthusiastic about everyone and everything. It's amazing how confident you will feel when you show enthusiasm and warmth to those around you. Think about how you act around others. Would you want to hang out with you?!

You can enjoy life much more if you let go of perfection and realize that you are who you are and others are who they are. If we want to see changes, we can only make them in ourselves.

It's also time to let go of the past. There is a story in the Bible about Lot and his wife.

They were told to leave the towns of Sodom and Gomorrah and to not look back. Lot's wife was so full of anguish that as she left the town, she looked back and was "frozen" into a pillar of salt. When we spend too much time looking back instead of forward we can be frozen, too.

All of us have experienced events which could give us a negative outlook on life. Start today to deal with anything that has happened, make any changes you need to make, and start looking positively forward to the wonderful life you can have!

Next Action:

Think about where you are at right now in your life. Which letter can you work on to build confidence? Look back at what you wrote in the Next Action section for each chapter.

Do you want more self-confidence and higher self-esteem? Pick a place to start—

C—Continue to Learn
O—Only You Can Change Anything
N—Notice Your Surroundings
F—Face Your Fears
I—Imagine the Best
D—Dare to Have Big Goals
E—Establish Systems
N—Never Give Up
C—Compare Yourself Only to Yourself
E—Enjoy Life!

Letter: _____

Action I'm going to take:

_____

_____

_____

Afterword

It's Your Time

Never trust how you feel on a daily basis. Trust the process, work your plan, and anything you want to achieve is possible. –Mark LeBlanc

Why should you get organized?

I recently helped a woman organize her husband's office. She is 50 years old. Her husband, age 52, had passed away two months earlier. This is not what we expect to happen in our lives at this age. Fortunately for my client, her husband was a very organized person and had all the family affairs in order. We went through his office together so that she would know where everything was and to set it up so that she could find anything she needed. As we laughed and cried together, I realized what a gift her husband had given her by having things in order before he died.

We never know what life is going to throw us. When you're organized and life throws you curve balls—and believe me, it will—you can handle them so much better.

Why should you get organized?

Why not just leave things like they are?

My question is, "How do you feel about yourself when you are in your home or office?"

I've found that when you're organized, an extreme sense of self-confidence shows up. You walk into situations feelings better about yourself. There's peace of mind and less stress. You save time. You save money. All kinds of great things happen.

You're open to more opportunities and things that can happen for you in your life, instead of worrying and fretting and closing yourself off to possibilities.

Good things can happen when you're organized.

May they happen to you.

Right now I'm going to:

_____

_____

CONFIDENCE IS ONLY AN ACTION STEP AWAY!

Appendix

Please download your free bonus chapter "Meet Me in the Kitchen Because Now I Love Being There!" at—

www.ElizabethHagen.com/bonuschapter

Basic Organizing Tools:

- Black trash bags
- Organizing signs from manual
- Room forms from manual
- Take Action form from manual
- Sharpie pens
- Zip-loc bags
- Clear Sterilite bins (6 qt and 15 qt)
- 18 gallon Rubbermaid bins
- Cardboard storage boxes from office supply store
- 3 × 5 cards

- 2″ × 4″ white labels
- Brother PTouch Labeler
- 2″ × 4″ white labels
- 18-gallon bins
- 6-qt. and 15-qt clear bins

Office
- Black trash bags
- Paper Tiger Software
  (www.SaveAnHouraDay.com)
- Hanging file folders (letter or legal depending on file drawers)
- Avery 5167 labels for Vital Files System
- Print out labels from manual and put in tab inserts
- Small spiral notebook for Purchases/Errands folder
- Follow-up forms from the manual
- Shredder

Home/Kitchen
- Black trash bags
- Black desk-top file holder
- Tickler File (www.TheTicklerFile.com) for

the Command Center
- One box letter-size yellow hanging file folders for Command Center
- HomeFile Financial Planning Kit (www.elizabethhagen.com/homeorganizing.html#fp)
- Interlocking drawer divider containers
- Post-it notes
- 1-1/2″ 3-ring binder for My Favorite Recipes binder
- 2 sets Avery Extra Wide Big Tab Insertable Dividers (EW2138) for the My Favorite Recipes binder
- Plastic page protectors for My Favorite Recipes binder
- My Favorite Recipe forms from the manual
- 1″ 3-ring binder for Family Notebook
- 2 sets Avery 8-tab Insertable Index Dividers for Family Notebook
- Family Notebook forms from the manual

Home/Closet
- Black trash bags
- Hangers

- 2-pocket folder
- Closet forms from the manual
- Plastic baskets/bins
- Interlocking drawer divider containers
- Box for alterations
- www.DressingWell.com—personal image, professional dress, and business casual resource

Invite Elizabeth Hagen to speak at your next meeting or event.

If you like the book, you will love having Elizabeth speak at your next meeting or event. She has the rare ability to take an ordinary gathering and turn it into a life-changing experience for those who hear her. From organizing your stuff to organizing your life, she draws upon personal and profound experiences that have helped her become successful in her life, work, marriage, and family. She walks the walk, and talks the talk! And now you can share her with your friends and colleagues. Book her today!

–Mark LeBlanc, Small Business Success
Author of *Growing Your Business!*

Organize with Confidence

Elizabeth conducts her signature presentation for home and office professionals who want to get more done and work less! Depending on your format, time available, and meeting objectives, her presentation can run from thirty minutes to an all-day workshop. The seminar focuses on the core issues which professionals face on a daily basis—more focus, a more organized home and office environment, and more productive time which equals a better quality of life!

For availability and booking information, you can reach Elizabeth at (605) 357-8767.

www.ElizabethHagen.com

Final Thoughts

1. Share **Organize with Confidence** with your friends, family members, and colleagues. Buy 50 copies and receive a 50% discount off the retail price. Call (605) 357-8767 for special pricing on larger quantities.

2. Send me your comments. I'd love to hear how this book has changed your life and any ideas you have for my future books. Mail or e-mail to:

Elizabeth Hagen
4400 Northridge Circle
Sioux Falls, SD 57105
Elizabeth@ElizabethHagen.com

3. Go to **www.ElizabethHagen.com** and subscribe to my FREE monthly newsletter "Extraordinary Results." You'll receive great inspiration, tips and resources on how to make your life better and you receive a gift from me!